Grandpa's Wisdom

SECRETS TO THE GOOD LIFE

J Blasiman

Cover photograph by Hilary Sievers
Cover design by Hilary Sievers

Copyright © 2014 Poised Affluence LLC
All rights reserved.
ISBN: 0615906125
ISBN 13: 9780615906126
Library of Congress Control Number: 2013954484
Grandpa's Wisdom, Columbus, OH

To Grandpa—
The voice of unconditional love and my guide in
this journey. With thanks for your wisdom, which has
always been one of the few things that has given
me strength when I couldn't get myself moving.

FOREWORD

This book is about life and how we choose to live it. We hope that after you read it, you will think about how your life is going. It is very interesting and may bring a tear to your eye once in a while. In the book, Jayme talks about her adventures in life and how she has chosen to handle them. What makes all of our lives better is love--unconditional love. Be sure to show and tell all of your loved ones how much you love them while they are still alive.

Jayme mentions all the things God and I have done to make her life better. I am so happy that I have been able to be an influence on her. Any time you can help someone, it makes you a better person. Grandma and I love her very much. Always remember that God can help us if we only ask, have patience, and allow him.

Wilbur "Grandpa" Blasiman

PREFACE

I am writing this book for one simple reason—to "pay it forward" by sharing my gift--I have been blessed to have witnessed an inspiring and healthy relationship between my grandparents on my father's side. Some people never have the opportunity to get to know or even meet their grandparents. Some people have not had the chance to witness a healthy relationship built on unconditional love, respect, and loyalty.

I have had both a close and loving relationship with my grandpa and I have personally experienced a deep, intimate relationship with my first true love and the mother of my children. As a result, I have had amazing and profound experiences and I would like to share them with you.

I want my children to read this book someday when they get older so they can understand what their last name represents. I want my children to read it and know that their parents' separation was no one's fault; it was just the end result of two people growing and learning.

Through this book, I want to honor my grandpa whom I refer to as "Yoda". Those of you who are familiar with *Star Wars* understand my analogy and know how much I believe in the lessons Grandpa has to teach, so much that

I have always believed that if I can be half the person he is, I will make this world a better place just by being here. He lives the example and teaches me about the person I aspire to become. I have chosen to explore the secrets to life, relationships, children, and family because I have witnessed Grandpa's character firsthand and I feel in my heart that Grandpa has successfully mastered these areas in life.

Many of us have had mentors and idols in our lifetimes. Most of the time, we are reminded of how human those mentors are by the mistakes they make or the times they let us down. I can write this next statement with complete conviction: Grandpa has *never* let me down. Sometimes I feel as if I should pinch him to make sure he is real. I am certain he is one of God's angels. Grandpa has been my lifeline.

Silent at times, but he has always been an active partner throughout my life—the angel on my shoulder, if you will. I want my daughter and son to learn Grandpa's life lessons. I want you, as the witness to my life, to have the opportunity to learn from this adventure and this journey. This book isn't meant to provide you with answers, but rather to give you the opportunity for self-appraisal and honest evaluation. Self-referral, looking within, is where true fulfillment begins...

———

I look in the mirror.
What do I see?

The almond-colored hair and my blue eyes…the fair skin that covers my bones.
Who am I looking at?
Who is looking back at me?

All the physical parts are there. It's just the interpretation of the whole picture that's missing. In many ways it's like slowly waking up from a deep sleep--I gradually come to an awareness of my surroundings and where I am at this very moment.

On some level or another, I am seeking myself, whether I believe it or not. I have beliefs, ideas, thoughts, and attitudes that govern my thinking, my knowing, and my living. Changing my thinking, my long-held beliefs, can dramatically change my daily life. A change has to happen before I fall deeper into darkness. I try looking at it this way: I'm feeling pain and I know it won't get any better unless I undertake a journey. I'm not sure where I'm going. But it is a place that you and I will travel together as I share my deepest thoughts and feelings in this book.

I wonder if you will take my hand and walk with me…

ONE

I splashed water over my face to wash away the tears and took another look in the mirror at my blue eyes. I saw Grandpa's eyes—staring back at me. My mind started racing again. I had so many questions, but the one that sent me on this journey was, "How did I get here?"

I went downstairs with my mind still reeling and reflecting. I drove to Blendon Woods, a wonderful park that Shay, the kids, and I would visit often. This time I would be taking the walk alone. It would be a walk filled with self-reflection and a long hard conversation with God. I stepped out of the car when I arrived and the brisk fall air nipped at my face.

Everything Always Works Out:

I was thirteen years old when my mom knocked on my bedroom door and came in to tell me she was going to be moving out. That she and Dad were going to separate. The news hit me like a ton of bricks. I can't remember if I even shed a tear then because I was numb and in shock. A few hours later after my mom left the house, I heard my dad walk past my room and into his bedroom. He began crying uncontrollably and I heard him punch the wall. I couldn't move—I was afraid. Not afraid of him harming me, but afraid of seeing my dad at one of the lowest moments of his life. I was afraid of seeing his pain, anger, and frustration.

It was a confusing and challenging time. I was getting migraine headaches and stomachaches. I wasn't myself. I descended into depression and withdrew from everyone. In the few months that preceded my parents' separation, I would go outside and play basketball in the rain, just to clear my head and cry. The rain would wash away my salty tears and the pain that filled them. Playing basketball in my driveway was my escape.

I felt as if I had lost everything. Everything I had ever known in my life was being turned upside down. I kept asking: Why were my parents being so selfish? What about my brother Scott and me? Where would we live? Would we have to stay with our mom on some days and with our dad on other days? What would Christmas be like? Christmas is meant to be about family and building family traditions. The most magical holiday for a child would now be transformed into the holiday I dreaded most because of awkward extended-family Christmas parties and the lack of family atmosphere.

The process to complete my parents' separation had been set in motion with the lawyers. More than three months prior, I was sitting in my bedroom with my door shut because our home did not feel like a home, but more like a battlefield. I was thirteen years old and carrying the weight of the situation on my shoulders. I was so confused. I did not understand how this could be happening to my family. I felt anger toward my parents. I felt betrayed. Why couldn't they tough it out?

The first lesson I remember internalizing from Grandpa was that everything always works out. I learned the truth of this lesson when I was attending summer school just before my sophomore year in high school. The teacher called Grandpa to come and pick me up because I wasn't feeling well. As I laid on his couch with a cool washcloth over my eyes, my thoughts were in a whirl.

Grandpa was standing next to me. "Jayme, how are you feeling?" he asked. I was short with my response--"I'm fine." I followed my abrupt answer by firing off some poisonous comments littered with undertones of ego-driven entitlement--"They are being so selfish. Why aren't they thinking about Scott and me? Why are they getting a divorce?" Grandpa took a deep breath and said, "Jayme, everything always works out. Everything will be OK." I felt so hurt, confused, and alone. I had a difficult time believing Grandpa.

Fast-forward twenty years--my parents, my brother, and I always have Christmas together. My parents live in Northeast Ohio. I live two hours away in Central Ohio, and my parents ride down together to attend my children's' birthday parties and events. It was true. As Grandpa said, everything always does work out. Maybe not how we initially expect, but God has his plan and things do fall into place.

As other challenges came up in my life, I often thought back to the conversation in my grandparents' living room on the afternoon Grandpa picked me up from summer school. Logically, I understood the words he had said to me, "Everything always works out", but emotionally I still did not understand how it would or could all work out.

There is something to be said about life experiences that come with age and the faith you build through those experiences. When I was thirteen years old, I did not have the experiences Grandpa had lived through, but his ability to believe was strong and I saw honesty and love in Grandpa's eyes. I decided to trust him.

Now I understand why and how Grandpa has such a strong belief that everything always works out. He simply puts it in God's hands and lets fate take its course. He knows that God's plans are far better than any plan he could create for himself. It is because of this belief that I believe he naturally attracts an abundance of love, happiness, and joy. As Rhonda Byrne explains in *The Secret*--even things that seem negative to us are all part of life's learning process:

> If you had had a perfect existence up until now, where everything had gone exactly right, you might not have a strong determination and desire to change your life. It's all of the apparently "negative" things that happen to us that give us a huge desire to change things. That huge desire that arises within you is like a magnetic fire, and it is very powerful.
>
> Be grateful for everything that caused that fire to ignite a massive desire within you, because that fire of

desire will give you strength and determination, and you will change your life.

Thinking back on Grandpa's words, I've asked myself what I would want my children, Jadyn and Jordyn, to learn from this lesson. I would want them to learn that even though they may not always understand what I am telling them, they can still open their hearts to trust. As much as I fought the acceptance of Grandpa's message because I did not understand how things would work out, I did trust and believe in Grandpa's wisdom and his unconditional love. My hopes are that Jadyn and Jordyn trust and believe in me like I do in Grandpa.

It is impossible for anyone to escape hardships. After my parents' separation, I thought there was no way for any sense of normalcy to return to my life, but it did all work out. As my life progressed, I faced a number of other challenges. It became clear to me that I would have pain in my life, but it was my choice whether or not I continued to suffer, or view it as a gift to grow.

Each time something came up that I thought I couldn't handle, Grandpa's wisdom rang true: "Everything will work out." It took over 20 years of life experiences to "know" these words to be true within myself. Every time I thought the worst thing had just happened and all was lost, somehow everything worked out.

———

As I walked the trails in Blendon Woods Park, remembering the times when I doubted that things could possibly work out, I gave myself a pep talk: *Just surrender*, I told myself. *Just let go. Let go and let God.* On that chilly fall day, I was staring at my own separation in the eyes, and I was feeling tested, yet again. Deep down, I knew everything would work out, but it was the silent, lonely nights that tested my belief in Grandpa's lesson.

Here I was in my early thirties, recently separated from the woman that I loved—the mother of my children. I felt as if I was being forced to live a life I did not want to live. I felt so ashamed to tell anyone that Shay and I had separated and that I had moved out. I felt I would be judged even more harshly because we were a same-sex couple with children.

Why did I leave? Why did I move out? I didn't know what to do or how to fix it. I was lost. When Shay told me she was not in love with me anymore, I felt as if my internal world just crashed down. Until that point, my family and my relationship had become my identity. *Who am I now without them? Who am I to become? What do I stand for? What will I not stand for?* These are all questions I could not answer three-and-half-years ago. I was empty. I could not find joy.

During those first few months after I moved out, I experienced the darkest moments of my life. Thoughts went through my head that I am not proud of. There were moments I questioned my purpose here on earth as I wondered if I needed to be here anymore. Many days I could not even bring myself to get out of bed.

With each passing day, in some ways it got easier. But in other ways, I felt the pain would never end. My life was different now--not being with Jadyn and Jordyn each day, not getting kisses from them each morning before I go to work—I thought it would never get easier. Jadyn asked frequently why I would not stay with her at home.

I felt like I had let down the three most important people in my life—Shay, Jadyn, and Jordyn During my walks in the park, I pondered—will Shay be able to forgive me for being emotionally numb for so long during our relationship and for causing the hurt that often comes with separating? I didn't know. What I did know was that I would continue loving even through the pain because I knew love was the greatest gift God had given me.

When I look at it now, I don't regret moving out three-and-half-years ago. That is where Shay and I were in our lives. It was the best decision for us as individuals. We were both lost and in a "damned-if-we-do, damned-if we-don't" situation. Prior to the implosion of my relationship with Shay, I felt that our relationship was starting a new positive chapter an upswing in our lives together. We had recently bought a new house together and were excited about the thought of Jadyn having a sibling.

The collapse of our relationship came to a head over a twelve-month period after a series of monumental events. In that time span, we found out that Shay, was pregnant with Jordyn; her father and grandfather both passed away; and Jordyn was born and diagnosed with a heart condition when he was a month old. Once the separation occurred, these were some of the darkest moments I have ever experienced in my life I spent many nights asking God what I had done so wrong to deserve all of this.

Why was everything being taken from me? Cancer took my father-in-law's (Tim's) life. Why had God taken him from us so soon? He was the first loss I had experienced in my adult life. He was supposed to meet and hold his grandson, who carries his name. I miss him. He was my friend, my "home-improvement buddy". Three months after we buried Tim, Shay's grandfather passed. Four months after he passed, our son, Jordyn was born.

It was a bittersweet moment when Jordyn Timothy Blasiman came into this world. Part of my heart was aching because I wished Tim could have been there to see our son and hold him. I felt so happy, yet part of me felt sadness and a sense of emptiness because the man Jordyn would have called "Papa" was missing. One month from the day "Bubba" (what we affectionately call Jordyn) arrived in this great big world, Shay and I took him to Nationwide Children's Hospital because he would not keep his food down and he was extremely lethargic.

We were new parents adjusting to our newest addition and we were still getting used to his different cries. When we arrived at the hospital, they took his vitals and rushed the three of us to critical care. His oxygen level was at 60 percent and his heart rate was 298. A normal heart rate for an infant is between 120 and 140. He was in what doctors refer to as SVT, or supraventricular tachycardia. Later he was diagnosed with Wolff-Parkinson-White syndrome, or WPW. In WPW syndrome, an extra electrical pathway between the heart's upper chambers and lower chambers causes a rapid heartbeat. WPW is detected in about four out of every 100,000 people.

I have never felt as helpless as I did when the doctors and nurses were working on Jordyn. The doctor explained to Shay and I how they were going to try and pull Jordyn out of SVT without using drugs. The doctor would place an ice bag over Jordyn's face temporarily with the goal of triggering Jordyn to bare down which would in turn slow his heart rate and bring him out of SVT. His little body just lay there with so many wires and tubes falling by his side. Wondering if we would take our son home again was one of the most helpless feelings in my life.

We had been told by the doctors that there was nothing that caused Jordyn to have WPW. We were told that it just happens. We returned to the emergency room two more times over the next three weeks. It took me over a year to say out loud that our son had a disability.

During the days and weeks after Jordyn's first diagnosis, I was so numb. I felt disconnected from my life. I spent my thirty-first birthday in the hospital with Shay and Jordyn. When we came home from that hospital visit, I started to become fearful of where my life was heading. The first night back, I went into Jordyn's room to say my prayers and rested my hand on his chest. I thanked God for not taking our son from us.

Then I remember pausing and thinking--*What is wrong with me?* I had just thanked God for not taking our son from us, but I didn't have tears in my eyes to match that emotion. I felt nothing. It was almost like I was on the outside looking in, asking myself, *Where are you, Jayme? Where have you gone? Why are you not feeling?*

I was in such a dark place. I had to find myself again. My whole world was falling apart around me. It was as if I were in a coma. I wanted so badly to be everything to Shay and the kids, but I could not talk, I could not move, I could not open my eyes. I could hear them talking to me. They were begging me to wake up for them, but I felt like a stranger to myself--just a shell. I just wanted and needed to find myself again, but I didn't know how to do it.

About two months after Jordyn was diagnosed with his heart condition, Shay and I separated after being together over seven years. She had fallen out of love with me and I had fallen out of love with myself. I moved out of our house and moved in with a friend. I wanted to be the partner and parent I knew I could be, but I didn't know how to save myself.

I was so frustrated with myself. How had I gotten to the point where I was completely disconnected from the core of who I am? It certainly had not happened overnight. I looked in the mirror and saw a stranger. This was when my true journey of self-discovery began. This is when I started to really "feel" Grandpa's lessons.

I have been told that motion creates emotion and emotion creates connections and love between people. This was my movement from understanding Grandpa's lessons logically to understanding them emotionally. For me, the key to learning any lesson and applying it is first understanding it logically and then making an emotional connection to it. I realized that I had been living my life unconsciously—without emotion or connection. Emotional awareness was the first step in my spiritual growth.

The more I tried to control, the more God let me know I was not supposed to control. I was just supposed to surrender and believe that everything would be OK. I did not listen for a long time. First Tim was taken from us, then Jordyn's heart condition rocked my world, and then I lost my first true love. God tried to get me to listen, but I would not surrender and set my spirit free. I needed to let go and believe that everything would work out.

———

In my journey through life, despite all my trials, everything always worked out. The key was holding on long enough to see everything through, allowing God to do his work, and having an open heart and mind to see and accept the work He was doing. I had to take it one day one at a time. I had to let go of the past and not worry too much about the future.

As much as I had gone through during this process, I recognized that the events of my life were necessary for me to become the woman I am today. The challenging events of that ten-month period, when I felt as if my life was falling apart, were blessings in disguise. These same events scared me into feeling and being present again.

I learned that I must not let fear dictate my actions because there are folks who love and care about me deeply. I learned I must do my best to maintain my belief that everything will work out. I learned I should not be attached to the outcome and that I should not focus on how it will work out. I learned that I should take it one day at a time because that is the true value of living in the moment.

It hurt to think about the past, so I did my best to stop focusing on it. I shifted gears and did what came naturally to me and started thinking about my future. However, that made me sad because my future was blank. It hurt to look back and it hurt to look forward. All I could do was focus on today and getting through. Some days were better than others, but that was OK! With each passing day, I kept telling myself, "It will all work out." Eventually, I started to develop belief and faith in my words.

I would wake up each morning and look myself in the mirror and say out loud, "Everything will be OK. Everything will work out." I didn't know how, but I kept repeating those words over and over again until they stuck. On the really tough days, I called Grandpa to hear him say those words to me--"Everything will work out, Jayme."

What really helped me let go of all those disempowering feelings? Many days, often multiple times in a day, I said quietly and sometimes out loud:

> "Thank you, God, for giving me the strength and courage to follow your path for me, the absolute faith to give you complete control and just let go, and the belief to know everything will be OK."

Eventually, I surrendered to love and thanked God for my pain. All pain is a lesson. It is a lesson God wanted me to learn.

I continued my walk down the trail and reflected. It was as if I were pressing the rewind button of my life with each step I took down the trail. Over the following three years, I would make many more trips to Blendon Woods Park.

TWO

Several months after my first contemplative walk in Blendon Woods, I was sitting by myself on a park bench along the side of the trail. I heard the wind blowing gently by my ears, the rustling of leaves, and the distant sound of laughter.

After a few moments in the stillness on the park bench, I fell into myself. It was as if I existed and didn't exist at the same time.

I heard the beating of my heart and the breathing in my lungs, and then it hit me--

I was alone.

Really alone—my only companion was myself as my mind played back my life experiences.

The Courtship:
Grandpa grew up during the economic and social whirl of The Depression. He was born on August 12, 1929— just two months shy of the stock market crash, when the Roaring Twenties came to an unceremonious halt. As a child, Grandpa had to help his parents on the farm before

and after school, but he and his parents understood the importance of a good education so he never left school. As he progressed through school, he continued to help out on the farm and the family tried to make ends meet with the thirty dollars a month that Grandpa's dad earned.

When he wasn't working or going to school, Grandpa pursued his passion for baseball. He played sandlot ball whenever he could and he dreamed of one day making it to the big leagues. Grandpa got a chance to try out for the Cleveland Indians, but unfortunately tough times required him to focus less on sports and more on school and work and he had to give up on his dream of baseball. In 1947 Grandpa was one of 30 students to graduate from his local high school. Shortly after he graduated from high school, something happened to Grandpa that would forever change his life-he fell in love.

In 1949, near Salem, Ohio, at a dance at Grange Hall called the "Good Time Party", Grandpa met a beautiful young woman named Donna Jean and became immediately enchanted. Grandpa was 21 years old and my grandma-to-be was 17. He later said of that moment that meeting her "was like being bitten by something". I asked Grandpa how he knew Grandma was "the one". His response was simple--"I just knew." He wanted to be with her. He could not get her out of his head. Grandpa just knew she was the gal he wanted to be with for the rest of his life.

As the courtship with Grandma progressed, Grandpa began to rethink what was truly important to him. His dream was no longer to play baseball or to pursue front-office work in baseball. In fact, he realized that the travel involved in working for the game he loved would take him away from the most important thing in his life. He couldn't bear being away from his love, Donna Jean. Grandpa always says, "Love changes everything." He could not be more right. I would even go one step further and say that love *is* everything.

Grandpa and Grandma courted for two years. Then something happened that not only shook Grandpa's life, but the world as well. As the Korean War flared up, the United States and the Soviet Union used the foreign conflict as a battleground to further escalate the Cold War. With the military stretched thin, Grandpa was drafted into the US Army in 1951. He said this was the only time in his life he ever truly knew the meaning of fear.

Like so many other young soldiers, Grandpa was forced to leave both the life he had made and the woman he loved. He said, "Leaving Donna was the hardest thing I ever had to do." When Grandpa was overseas, he and Grandma would write each other almost every day.

I can recall a conversation I had with Grandpa that brought home to me just how much he and Grandma were in love: It had been about two years after Shay and I separated and nine years since Grandma was first diagnosed with Alzheimer's. Grandpa and I were standing in their bedroom in front of Grandma's jewelry box. Grandpa looked up at me and said, "Jayme, this is Grandma's jewelry box. She has had it almost as long as you have been alive. Would you like to have it?" With amazement I responded, "I would love to have it!"

Just like a little kid, I started opening every door and drawer. In one of the drawers a silver bracelet caught my attention. I picked up the bracelet and saw "ISALYS" engraved on it. "What does 'ISALYS' stand for?", I asked Grandpa. Grandpa explained that when he was overseas for over a year that they both put "ISALYS" at the end of every letter they wrote to each other.

As Grandpa explained this to me, I held the bracelet in my hand and started to understand how much this bracelet meant to both him and Grandma. Grandpa gently reached over and picked the bracelet up out of my hand. He admired the engraved letters on it. As happy and grateful tears filled his eyes, he uttered the words, "I Shall Always Love You, Sweetheart."

Grandpa's feelings for Grandma reminded me of the first time I met Shay. I was a district manager for an international marketing firm and I was interviewing candidates for the sales positions. Many days I would run interviews and train new hires during the same day. It was one of those typical days when I met Shay for the first time. I looked up as she walked into my office. When I looked at her, I lost all concentration. She was gorgeous and I was very attracted to her. After our first conversation, I knew she was going to be in my life for a very long time.

During the interview, I offered Shay a position and she accepted. A few days later, a group of coworkers and I (including Shay) went by the river in downtown Columbus to take in the beautiful scenery. After the group returned to the office, I did not want Shay to go home, so I literally drove circles around her in the parking lot so she could not get in her car. After that night we continued our courtship and within a few weeks we moved into an apartment together.

———

When my parents divorced, I didn't know how to put the pieces together. I simply wanted to disappear. Yet in all honesty, I also wanted to be reassured that I was loved. I wanted that same reassurance years later when I went through my own separation.

Who wants to be alone and afraid?

Who wants to feel as though she is no longer significant to someone they were in love with?

It was as if I were standing over a cliff. I couldn't judge the depth—was it three or thirty feet deep?

Would anyone catch me if I fell? That's the most important question, isn't it? Would anyone know, or care, if I fell?

I felt so alone.

I didn't care what people said; being alone and feeling lonely was crushing. It felt like a heavy weight had been set upon my shoulders and I could hardly move. The feeling would sneak up on me. Then there were other times I'd think I was OK and I thought I was going to make it. Then I would hear a song or see a couple holding hands and loneliness would descend upon me again and I would drift into a cloud of nothingness. I could hardly breathe—I was paralyzed.

Nighttime was the hardest part of the day. I would lie in bed as if someone were piling dirt on my coffin. I couldn't wait for daytime. Months after I moved out, I still found myself often lost in thought. I scrutinized every aspect of my life and analyzed every waking moment as if the answer were somewhere obvious, right in front of me. *Why was I losing everything? Why was my family falling apart?*

The separation from Shay felt like having a piece of me ripped away—as if part of my identity had been stolen from me. *What will this feel like a year from now?* I wondered. Maybe next year it would be just a dull ache but this year it hurt to breathe.

———

As I sat on my lonely park bench, I remembered the sensual, ecstatic thrill of total trust and intimacy I once had with Shay. I knew she still existed, but it was as if she were in a different dimension, getting farther and farther away. I felt guilt. *Am I the betrayer?* I wondered.

I was dealing with so many losses all at the same time and the pain layered on top of me. I was hurting from a broken heart and a lost relationship. My heart was in pain. I felt betrayed, though I was not sure by whom.

There were so many changes connected with my separation. I had changed where I lived, how I spent my day, what I could afford to do, how much time I spent with my children and when, and how I planned for the future all while trying to deal with a whole new world of loss. The process of grieving began to set in.

Whether I liked to admit it or not, there was still a sense of shame connected with all this. I felt like a failure.

I didn't want to feel this way. I explored the questions of how to make sense of it all and how to rebuild. Yet through everything, I heard Grandpa's voice in my heart and soul reminding me to let go and let the universe do its work.

THREE

A spring morning about a year and half after Shay and I separated, I set out on another journey down the park trail at Blendon Woods. During my walk I began to feel the whole me—the child, the woman, the lover, the parent, the breadwinner—yet it all melted away. There is only one me. Dice me up, chop me into pieces, turn me into a million grains of sand--in the end, it is all *ME*; a person who needs love.

   Not a convenient or contrived love, but that honest, unconditional love that Grandpa so simply allows to drift from his being like a favorite song, familiar and comforting. Could it be that that love had always been there just waiting for me to embrace it? Like a child's favorite teddy bear that has been placed on the shelf for too long? Maybe I just needed to reach out and find it.

A Celebration of Life:

Grandpa's mother was taken from him suddenly. One day she complained about having chest pains and they rushed her to the emergency room. The doctor announced shortly after arriving at the hospital that she had passed. She was only 65 years old and Grandpa was 46.

Just as Grandpa's three sons, Gary, Gerald, and Doug, are a reflection of their parents, Grandpa is a reflection of the extraordinary woman he called Mom. She is an important reason Grandpa turned out the way he did. Although they did not have much growing up during the Depression, his mother gave him as much as she could and did so selflessly.

Grandpa explained during one of our conversations that when he lost his mother, it solidified and reinforced a belief that he already had. He understood that life is a precious gift and that the time spent with loved ones is also precious; that each moment should be valued and savored.

He has carried this mind-set with him to the present. Every morning he talks to God and thanks Him for all his blessings. He prays for his friends and family and trusts the Lord to look after them. When Grandma became ill, he also asked God to bless him with health so he could care for Grandma who had Alzheimer's. As our family continues to grow, Grandpa said that he hopes to continue teaching his great-grandchildren honesty, respect, a positive mind-set, and a belief in the Higher Power.

Remembering loved ones who have passed keeps them alive for all the good they taught us not only about the world, but also about ourselves. Grandpa told me, "Remember them. They will always be a big part of your life, no matter what, even if they have passed away."

I was there the day that the doctor told Shay and her parents that Tim's cancer was spreading. Shay was pregnant with our first child. We tried getting pregnant sooner so that our daughter could know her "Papa" (what Jadyn called Shay's dad). Shay had to leave the meeting with the doctor before they were done because she was so upset. As we sat on a bench in the hallway, I held her as she cried in my arms.

A few moments later, Shay's mom and dad came out. Her mom was crying, but Tim was not. The first thing Tim did was go to Shay and say in a stern fatherly voice, "Stop crying, Boo! You have to be healthy and not be stressed during your pregnancy." Tim's primary concern was for Shay and the baby, not himself—a reflection of his character.

After leaving the meeting with the doctor, Tim and I made our way to the condo to continue working on finishing the basement. We did not say much to each other. We just enjoyed each other's company, listened to jazz, and worked on putting framing together. I asked him if he was scared, and he said he was. He still kept a good spirit and positive attitude as we worked.

It was the second Thanksgiving since Shay and I separated. I spent the day after Thanksgiving, Black Friday, shopping with Grandpa. We ran into someone Grandpa knew from church. Grandpa asked the woman if she had attended the funeral service for a person they had both known. The woman told Grandpa she'd been unable to attend, so Grandpa told her what a wonderful service it was. He described it as a service that was a true celebration of the deceased's life. As I listened to Grandpa speak, I could not help but think that this is what he would want for Grandma. He would want her life celebrated, not mourned. I realized then that Grandpa is able to find the blessings even in death.

I've asked Grandpa about his views on death several times in recent years. He said he wants his passing to be a celebration of life. He wants people to talk about all the fun times and the memories they made together. He believes the best way to honor someone's life is through celebration and laughter, so he wants his family to throw a party when he dies. He made it a point to say that it is normal to be sad, but that you should never allow yourself to slip into a depression when someone passes.

He says depression robs you of your ability to operate out of a place of love. It robs your spouse, children, and family of your presence. Grandpa said he does not want anyone to become depressed when time on this earth is done for him and Grandma.

I asked him how he has handled the passing of his parents and some of his siblings without becoming depressed. He said there is no point in being depressed because we have no control over death. Life must and will go on even after someone passes. He only focuses on what he can control--he can choose either to celebrate the person's life or to be depressed. His choice has always been to enjoy the celebration of life. He believes it is critical to move on--miss them, love them, remember them, but keep living and be alive.

Grandpa believes that one of the best ways to keep living after a loved one passes away is to start or add to your bucket list of things you want to do before you die. Grandpa has a bucket list he adds to, even at 84 years old. Death is not a bad thing, but an opportunity for the living to celebrate the life that the deceased person lived and a chance for the deceased to walk hand in hand with God.

As I listened to Grandpa explain his views on death, I realized that passing away gave Tim a whole new freedom. It gave him freedom from all the pain his cancer was causing him and it gave him wings to watch over us. I realized how selfish I was, feeling sad because he was not here with us, instead of focusing on the wonderful gifts he had blessed this world with. I was only focusing on what I did not have, not on celebrating the gifts Tim had given.

There was no better example of celebrating Tim's life than our daughter, Jadyn. Less than two months after Tim passed away, Shay and I had laid Jadyn down to bed after we all said our prayers together. Shay and I went into our bedroom and turned on the baby monitor. As we were getting ready for bed, we heard Jadyn laughing out loud. Shay and I shared a puzzled look.

Jadyn was laughing with the deep belly laughs, amazing and infectious, that you typically hear from children. After listening to this for a few minutes, Shay and I went into Jadyn's room. She was still laughing as she looked up at us. I asked Jadyn, "Jady bug, what are you laughing at?" She looked at me with her big bluish-green eyes and a big smile on her face and said, "Papa is tickling me." Shay and I looked at each other with amazement. Shay's eyes started to fill with tears. We smiled at Jadyn. I said, "Don't stay up too late playing."

We all have something to learn from children. At two years old, Jadyn was completely present with Tim's spirit months after he passed. She was not scared. She was not crying. She was laughing and sharing joy with her Papa. She was celebrating his life even after his passing.

———

No one ever has a problem dealing with happiness or feeling good. When joy comes into our lives, we experience it freely, but when sadness or grief is present, we often struggle. This is especially true because we are always expected to be cheerful and have fun. We live in a culture that tells us to put on a happy face and hide our tears, which can make it difficult to be comfortable with sadness and grief.

Yet these emotions are a normal part of life. I have felt both with a vengeance. Whether they are caused by a situation such as mine, or a small everyday setback, I can learn to walk hand-in-hand with difficulties with greater ease because of my belief in Grandpa's lessons.

Not only can I become more at ease with these feelings thanks to Grandpa, but I can learn how to handle them in a healthy way, as this is also vital to my health and well-being. I learned that if I want to have a healthy emotional life, I need to honor all of my emotions and allow them room for expression. When sadness comes, I need to allow myself to feel it fully. It helps to understand that it is a normal, natural reaction to loss and not an indication that there is something wrong with me.

For me, personally, the only tragedy would be if I were to allow myself to fall into a depression. I would rob my children of my presence with them. I would rob the deceased of their celebration of life. I know that how I feel about any situation, or towards any person, depends 100 percent on what I choose to focus on and the meaning I place on the events.

FOUR

On this spring day it was getting close to sunset and I had already wandered in the park lost in thought for 45 minutes, but I continued down the trail; with each passing thought in my head, I reflected on Grandpa's lesson. I came to a fork in the trail. Should I go left or right?

Count Your Blessings:
Grandpa shared a story with me that drove this message home--

One day a nurse came to my grandparents' house to tend to Grandma. Grandpa observed that the nurse looked distraught and down. He found out that the nurse's husband had been laid off from work. Grandpa asked her how her husband's health was and she replied that he was well. He then asked her about the health of her children and she replied that they were also well. Grandpa asked her how her job was going and she responded once more that her job was going quite well.

"Sounds like you have a lot to be happy and thankful for," Grandpa said.

The nurse smiled, moved by Grandpa's perspective on life and said, "I always feel better after I have been here."

———

Sometimes the world passes me by so quickly that the stress and worry of tomorrow can make me forget what is truly important in life. The fact is both negative and positive surround me each day, but it is my choice on which I focus. I must determine my focus by asking myself questions such as: Are the negative things really negative or are they gifts from God? What if I changed my story? In this vein, I have asked myself: What if I changed the meaning I placed on my separation? Instead of focusing on the feelings of loss, shame, and failure, what if I looked at my separation as a gift and searched for the lessons I needed to learn?

I know it can be challenging to focus on only the positives in life, but asking myself these questions has helped me feel at a deeper, more emotional level instead of only at a commonsensical, logical level. At times in my past, it was hard to see how all that happened had been a blessing in some way. It was challenging to keep my heart open and my "internal light" on. Yet I knew I had to go on and push forward. I could not give up. I am a Blasiman and as Grandpa and Grandma always told me, "Blasimans do not say *can't* or give up. We just haven't figured it out yet".

Now as I wandered down the shady paths of Blendon Woods, I asked myself, "How do I snap myself out of the negative and self-pity talk? Maybe I should write myself a nasty tough-love letter once in a while where I can tell myself—that this is *enough*!" I decided I would not rob myself of any more freedom, joy, and happiness! It is OK to have tough days and experience sadness during those times. What is NOT OK is if I were to allow myself to be stuck there. It is encouraging to know that nothing lasts forever. Why would I want everything to be the same? Change brings growth and evolution. It has brought "the evolution of Jayme".

Every day I remind myself to stop trying to "get in the driver's seat". God is the driver, not me. When my focus changes from what I think I deserve but don't have to how I can serve, the world that surrounds me changes. The moment I am in is no longer a struggle. So, how can I serve? It is time for me to stop stumbling through life merely as a consumer looking for my "next fix". It is through serving and giving that we receive. I have to push through and continue focusing on my blessings. Appreciation of what I have brings what I want.

It took *the gift* of losing everything to realize what I had. Jadyn and Jordyn make my heart sing. I have a level of appreciation for being a parent to them that I would never have had if I had not experienced *the gift*. I have a desire to be the best wife I can possibly be for my future wife that I would never have had if I had not experienced the separation from Shay.

Facing the biggest, most painful challenges in life, I received my greatest gifts and lessons in life. I have moved out of the darkness and into light. I moved out of my head and into my heart. I have learned what true love is and that what I was searching for was in me all along. I understand now that Shay and I do not have to be intimately involved or be together to share each other's love for our children.

I must remember to keep counting my blessings. It is time to change my focus to "how can I serve?" I am at a fork in the path. Which path am I going to choose? What am I going to choose to focus on? The quality of my life is found in the meaning I place on events. Life is not the challenges that I face, but the meaning that I give to these challenges.

———

I was startled when I heard rustling in the woods about twenty feet off the park trail. I looked to my right and there were two wild turkeys. I stopped and watched them. I recalled some of the walks Shay and I, and later Jadyn, had gone on together. I snapped back to the present and continued my journey down the trail.

FIVE

Parenting is a mix of discipline and love that creates a close, loving family:
In 1961, Grandpa and Grandma decided together that Grandma would go to college to get a degree. This was a decision that required sacrifice from the whole family as she would have to be away from her home and her children in order to do so. In a time when women were expected to stay at home with the children, Grandma challenged the norm. Her parents thought for sure that she and Grandpa were going to ruin their sons' lives since she was not staying at home to raise them. While Grandma was at class during the day, the boys stayed with Grandpa's mom.

On August 20, 1965, four years after beginning college, Grandma graduated with a degree from Youngstown State University. Despite their opposition, Grandma's mother and father were among the proudest parents at a graduation dominated by men. She later went on to get her master's degree in education from Kent State University. She was a true pioneer for her generation and Grandpa supported her every step of the way.

Aside from everything Grandma did for her family, earning two college degrees proved to be one of Grandma's greatest achievements. Grandma went on to have a purposeful career as a teacher shaping the lives of children. By the time she retired after thirty years of teaching, she had received numerous awards, including Teacher of the Year.

As a teacher, Grandma showed the same love for her students that she did for her family. She believed that a loving environment was a learning environment. Grandpa shared a story with me about Grandma. She was a third grade teacher at Goshen Elementary school. A little girl entered Grandma's class about half-way through the school year. She was a little behind compared to her peers in class.

The little girl's mother and Grandma decided that the mother would bring the little girl to school early so Grandma could work with her. By the end of the school year Grandma was able to bring her up to speed and current with her peers. Grandma made such an impression on the little girl and her mother that when Grandma retired six years later they made a special trip to visit Grandma on her last day. They brought her a cake and a thank you card to show their appreciation for all Grandma had done for the little girl.

As a child when I was in town with my grandparents, we would often run into some of Grandma's old students. I would see grown men and women turn into third graders again when speaking to her. I could sense how much they all respected her. It almost seemed as if she were royalty. As a child I remember thinking it was so cool—she was *my* grandma.

I am now thirty-five years old and finally know what I want to be when I grow up. I want to be a teacher just like Grandma. I want to teach people and give them the tools to help and inspire their relationships and help them save their families from separating. My classroom may not be in a school building like Grandma's classroom, but I can still carry on the teaching legacy that she started. Her contribution to this world is immeasurable with all the lives she has touched and affected. My hope is to do the same.

For Grandpa, a successful and fulfilling life has meant a good relationship with both his spouse and his children. This means appreciating each of them to the fullest each day of his life.

When I was interviewing Grandpa for this book, he told me that the births of his three boys were among the most amazing things that happened to him. We are all taught in our society that having children should feel and be amazing, but at that time, I did not have any yet. I had that conversation with him almost four years before my daughter was born. Writing this now, I know that back then I did not truly understand why he counted the births of his three boys among his proudest achievements.

———

Mati (Mah'-tee) is the Croatian word for mother. Shay and I agreed that the kids would call me "Mati" so they could distinguish between us. We picked this word because it means mother, yet it varies enough from "mommy" or "mom" to prevent confusion. Mati has become one of the most significant words in my life. I say this next sentence with absolute conviction and with tears of joy running down my cheeks: the proudest accomplishment of my life has been having my two children and becoming the parent I am today and continue striving to become. Initially, I wished for my family to be together, but that was not God's plan. It was God's plan for Shay and I to meet, fall in love, and have two amazing children together, and eventually separate.

I realized now that my family did not need the biggest, best, or most expensive "things." They just needed me! They needed me physically, mentally, spiritually, and emotionally. Now I make it a point to give Jadyn and Jordyn all that they deserve and the woman I marry will have all of me as well. At one point I thought I was too late to give those things to my family because we were separated, but that could not be further from the truth. I realized that I can give myself to Jadyn and Jordyn physically, mentally, spiritually, and emotionally just as I do now despite our current situation.

About a year and a half after I moved out, my daughter Jadyn asked, "Why is our family not together?" I told her, "Honey, God has some lessons that Momma and Mati need to learn". With tears running down her four-year-old face, she asked, "When is our family going to be together again?" I told her, "Our family is together now." Jadyn said, "We are not together because you are not at home with us and mommy." I looked into my daughter's bluish-green eyes and told her, "Our family will always be together as long as we keep loving one another. What keeps a family together is unconditional love."

———

Grandpa taught me that children are simply a reflection of their parents' actions and attitudes. If you want to see a true reflection of someone's personal fortitude, look at his or her young children. Grandpa and Grandma were blessed to have three boys, Gary, Gerald, and Doug. Gary was the eldest and Doug the youngest.

Some couples have a difference of opinion about how to raise children. Both Grandma and Grandpa decided that regardless of their personal beliefs, neither one would undermine the other in front of the boys, especially when the subject of discipline arose. Any difference of opinion was discussed in private.

Grandpa demanded a lot from his boys. According to Grandpa, "if you start discipline early, you won't have to discipline often". While he did discipline his children, he did it with love and respect as he saw it as a necessary aspect of child rearing. Out of respect for his children, Grandpa never disciplined the boys in front of other people. He did not want them to be embarrassed and lose sight of the lesson he was trying to teach.

He also recognized that too much punishment might drive the boys away. Grandpa has always said, "Love, above all else, beats out everything." Finding that happy medium between teaching a lesson through discipline and teaching a lesson through love and reasoning is a challenge for any parent, but Grandpa knew the best way to get his point across.

Approval and high regard lie at the heart of raising happy, well-adjusted children. Children are approval-seeking creatures. They crave love and appreciation. It is often difficult for a child to figure out the expectations of a parent that can range from strict discipline to insightful teachings.

One day when he was a kid, Doug shot out a garage door window with the boys' BB gun. Instead of running from the truth, he went to Grandpa and confessed the deed. Rather than punish him, Grandpa rewarded him for honesty because he recognized that it took courage to come and tell the truth. Positive reinforcement can often teach a much better lesson than negative punishment.

Honesty and integrity are traits Grandpa has always believed were of utmost importance, so he tried to instill those virtues in his children. No matter what they were doing, Grandpa wanted his boys to be true to others and to themselves. He taught them to finish what they started and to keep their heads up, no matter how bleak the outcome appeared. He taught them to never give up. He helped them understand that it wasn't that they could not do it, but rather that they just had not figured it out yet.

Grandpa built trust with his children which allowed them to bring their frustrations and challenges to him, but he also realized that a parent can sometimes only be there to offer guidance. Grandpa knew that to grow as individuals, his children needed to learn to take care of their own problems.

I would like my children to grow up internalizing the same lessons that Grandpa taught his sons. In the wake of my separation, I am especially interested in helping them develop resilience and the sense that they can handle their own problems. Jadyn and Jordyn are young—they may not quite understand why their parents separated.

They will each deal with it in their own way and any difficulties they have accepting our separation will manifest in them as they grow older. Separation is hard on parents and children alike. Children don't come with how-to manuals, neither do the situations I may encounter in life and as a parent, but I believe approval and high regard lie at the heart of raising happy, well-adjusted children.

———

During the week I get Jadyn and Jordyn on Tuesdays and Thursdays and I cherish my time with them. But right now, right this very minute, on a Wednesday, I wonder what they're doing, what they're thinking. Do they miss me? I just want to hold them. The biggest help I can give my children as they grow older and begin to understand the relationship between their parents is to remain open to them emotionally and to keep giving an abundance of love.

Grandpa always talked about unconditional love— I've come to rely on the warmth and comfort of his words and I make it a point to pass on that warmth and comfort to my children.

I need to trust myself and remember that the best way to help my children through the separation is for me to stay healthy and open to love. I need to believe that I am going to make it and that somewhere down the road, though maybe not today or tomorrow, my family, my children, and I will end up stronger, healthier, and happier for having gone through this profound event.

Do you love me, Mati? I don't want my children to ever have to ask this question. I want them to always know that I love them from the minute they wake up in the morning to the instant they drift off to sleep. I want to "slay the dragons in their dreams" and fight the monsters in the closet. I want to be there always and eternally in their hearts. I can't help but think about playing games with Jadyn or caressing Jordyn's cheek and gently running my fingers through his curly hair as he falls asleep in my arms. I know that tonight I can't kiss them good-night, but I can still provide the unconditional love that will be the foundation of their life.

Maybe that's the toughest part of God's lesson—waking up at night in the darkness, clutching my pillow with all my might, for an instant imagining I'm holding Jordyn or Jadyn when they cry out for me—but being all alone. Tears come easily then. Then I think about my parents. Am I a fool to believe that I am not like them in some way? In many ways, I am my parents—the good, the bad, and the beautiful—all in one package that is me. Am I the person I want my children to model?

Isn't that the question many parents ask themselves at one point or another while raising their children? I am proud of who I am and my family. YES--I am a person I want Jadyn and Jordyn to model.

SIX

I had reached the halfway point on the trail. I stopped at a bridge and watched the water pass under it. I was reminded of another of Grandpa's lessons...

Water Under the Bridge:

During the same summer conversation about my parents' separation when I was thirteen, I learned another valuable lesson: "water under the bridge." In other words, what is done is done, and we cannot change the past, so there is no need to live in it. As I recall the happenings of that afternoon, I don't remember what exactly I was talking to Grandpa about. I do know I was telling him about the sense of injustice and anger I had toward my mom and my dad, his son. He kept telling me, "Jayme, it is water under the bridge." He was trying to teach me that I had to let things go and not hold a grudge.

That summer afternoon sitting on my grandparents' couch so many hateful words came out of my mouth. For every negative comment I made, Grandpa would counter with a positive. I must have worn him down with all my poison because I looked up into his crystal-blue eyes and they filled with tears. I had never meant to make him cry or to hurt him, but I had so much anger, hurt, and pain flowing through me. I had hurt my angel; I had hurt Grandpa--the person who has one of the purest loves to have graced this earth.

How could I have such a selfish, dark side to me?

I was showing the side of me that's visible when I operate from my ego, or when I don't get what I think I deserve. No good ever comes from the ego. I have heard people say that EGO is an acronym that stands for "Edge God Out." The fulfillment I seek in life is rooted in faith and patience. I must operate from a place of love and service or I will poison the world around me.

As a teenager, I guess I hadn't learned yet how to just let things go. It's twenty years after that day in my grandparents' living room and I am still building my "forgiveness muscles". I am forgiving. Not only am I forgiving, but I have also intellectually and emotionally grasped what true forgiveness is--"giving up the hope that the past could have been any different".

Letting go is a choice and it means not holding the mistakes of the past over someone's head in the present. It also means not holding pain and resentment in my heart. Holding on to pain and anger prevents me from being open to other people. If my heart is filled with resentment, there is no space in my heart for love.

I realize now that my parents did the best they could. As it turned out, the healthiest thing for our family was for the two of them to part ways and become co-parents to finish raising my brother and me. To this day we still have

Christmas together as a family and my parents get along better than ever. Life is too short for us to hold grudges and not share magical family moments together.

Practicing forgiveness and just letting go...what an amazingly simple concept! Yet in practice, forgiveness has proven to be a challenge for me in areas of my life. I know I am not the only one in this world who has been hurt and who has struggled with forgiving someone who hurt me, but...

About six months after Shay and I separated, I asked Grandpa for his advice about forgiving people. He told me it is a must! If you don't forgive, you will carry a huge burden on your shoulders. By forgiving, I am helping not only the person who hurt me, but also myself. He went on to tell me that life is too short to carry such a large burden--"turn the baggage over to God and let him take care of it". I told Grandpa I understood what he was saying in theory, but I was struggling to forgive. I thought he was telling me that forgiveness should be easy, but that was my misinterpretation.

He told me that it will take time; that I had to be patient and gentle with myself. He told me that I have to focus on my blessings; to focus on love instead of reliving and thinking about how or why I was hurt. What if I dropped the baggage filled with pain? What if I walked up to God and handed him my baggage? What if I lit the bags on fire? Wouldn't I be free from my pain then? I was the one choosing to carry the baggage. It was time for me to make a new choice.

———

It had been about a year and a half since the separation. I stood on the bridge and watched the water pass under it. Some days I wondered how or if I will be able to let go and forgive myself and Shay. The big question I kept trying to answer is how do I forgive? I knew I did not want to carry this burden on my shoulders, but how was I supposed to forgive?

It was hard for me to believe that I could do so. I guess that was all part of the process of receiving God's gift to me. When I started to slip back into sadness and depression, I tried to do my best to focus on my blessings. But I noticed my focus had still been on what Shay did or didn't do for me. I thought about what I didn't have. Yet I needed to stop empowering my past. I was doing it at the expense of my destiny.

Was I crying because that is what I was supposed to do? Maybe I screamed because I missed my kids, but mainly I wondered what would become of me. Sometimes forgiveness isn't as easy as it sounds, especially when the person you do not want to forgive is yourself.

My walls were closing in and internally I was in shambles. The only thing I could have done is work at forgiving myself. It was hard work, but I knew I was healing me and my soul. I was getting aligned and becoming the best version of me by not placing blame on anyone or anything. I worked on owning my part of our separation, as well as working at forgiving myself and Shay.

———

After we had our chat, Grandpa and I went on to discuss how my generation had been conditioned to receive and achieve most things in a short time frame compared to when he was growing up. I had to admit, I felt he was right. I am accustomed to getting things done quickly. That is the world we live in today. We all want everything "done yesterday". If it doesn't get accomplished quickly, we either get upset or move on past the task or issue to something else without fully resolving the issue at hand.

Immediately after talking with Grandpa on the topic of forgiveness, I started a list of all the things I had that I was truly and deeply thankful for. Afterward, I noticed my posture changed, and I went from feeling hurt and depressed to feeling as if my heart was overflowing with love and joy. This all happened within a matter of moments.

It is human nature to want to avoid or move away from pain, but I felt in my heart that the best thing I could do for myself was to face the pain and fear and to look straight at it. Throughout my life, I've gotten better and faster at forgiving. This was challenging to apply, but I had to be persistent and keep practicing.

I often reminded myself: "To master forgiving I must practice, practice, and practice more! Like an Olympic athlete who practices her whole life for her competitions. She did not become an elite athlete in her event or sport overnight. It took a lot of practice. The more I practiced forgiving those that I felt had hurt me, the better I was getting at it. It was becoming part of my character.

SEVEN

Keep Practicing and Never Give Up:
The 1930's through the 1950's was an era of barnstorming baseball games and warm summer nights that evoked such passion and such a large following that it the game became known as "America's Favorite Pastime". The swing music of the era was clear and brash, like the music played by Benny Goodman's or Artie Shaw's bands. Men and women dressed to the hilt.

Despite the glamour of the era, it was also a simple time when values were forged through the Great Depression and it was a time when a person's word was his bond, a smile was simply a smile, and a handshake was a contract that lasted a lifetime. Every boy wanted to play ball and grow up to be Babe Ruth, Ty Cobb, Lou Gehrig, or a thin kid from the Midwest named Bob Feller.

Bob Feller was a famed pitcher for the Cleveland Indians who spent twenty years playing baseball. He played from the 1930's through the 1950's with time off only to serve in the Navy for four years during World War II. He was one of the best pitchers to ever grace the pitcher's mound for the Tribe. His fastball had blazing speed and his knowledge of the game was unsurpassed.

He was known to spend hours practicing his pitches and studying his opponents' strengths and weaknesses until he just instinctively knew how to pitch to any given player. When a batter came to the plate, he knew everything about that particular player. Bob knew what type of pitches the batter usually hit and the type he struggled with. It took practice, a lot of practice, to become Bob Feller.

You're probably wondering what this history lesson has to do with Grandpa's wisdom. Actually it's a critical part of the story. Grandpa taught me many lessons through baseball analogies since he loved baseball so much. He particularly loves the Cleveland Indians.

When asked to relate some of the key components of living, Grandpa said it takes practice, just like it did for his idol, Bob Feller. Creating the life you love living is about creating empowering patterns and practices in your life. Whether your job is to strike out a major-league batter, or to open your heart or learn to forgive, it all takes practice. It doesn't come naturally, but if you do it long enough, it does become second nature. If anything about Grandpa seeps into my heart and soul, it is how effortless it is for him to keep his heart open to love and forgiveness.

Grandpa doesn't worry about things he cannot change, or fret about what could have been; instead, he enjoys and celebrates each moment of his life, no matter what the current circumstances. He lives in the present. He enjoys and drinks up every moment. As he cared for Grandma through her illness, each caress of his hand upon her face, each kiss upon her cheek, and each kind word whispered in her ear were his testaments to true love.

He could have been angry at God for having this happen to his beloved, but instead he embraced each moment and cherished each second he spent with her. It is a testament to the human spirit's capacity to surpass pain when we give ourselves to love, rather than bask in fear, anger, and resentment. This is how I grow, holding on to Grandpa's example. I hear his voice is in my ear and feel his love in my heart in all that I do and say. If I need a refresher, it's still just a phone call away--for now.

Grandpa told me many times about the importance of persistence. My dad had been out of work for about eight months due to the economic downturn in 2008. Grandpa told me he had been praying for many months for my dad to get a job, but he also kept counting his blessings and focusing on empowering thoughts about what he wanted for my dad instead of focusing only on the fact that my dad did not have a job. Like Grandpa, when I was struggling, it was my choice to focus on my blessings and what I wanted, instead of focusing on what I didn't have.

On the challenging days, sometimes I felt like I didn't deserve to feel joyful again. I felt haunted by angry words, selfish actions, and things I could or should have done to improve my relationship with Shay. Sometimes I felt like it was a bad dream I could not wake up from. I prayed for strength and guidance to make the right decisions.

Sometimes it was easier for me to feel unworthy as if I was expecting lightning from heaven to strike me down. But I had to live with all the memories, thoughts, and emotions, and somewhere along the way, I had to find the path that would empower me.

I didn't want to go back to the way I was. I knew I could not change the past, but I was sure as hell not going to let the past determine my future. That was Grandpa's lesson about "water under the bridge". I had to let go. Still, although I had read quotes and books, listened to CDs and to Grandpa, letting go was not easy for me. Yet I persisted. I knew I needed to let go of hurt, anger, resentment, and frustration. I knew that if I let go, I would be gracing myself with freedom and clarity of mind.

Forgiveness is something Grandpa talks about with great passion. Without it, we risk robbing ourselves of our true passions and ambitions. A common saying that makes sense to me is "forgive and forget." I have heard many people say they will forgive but not forget. I suppose not forgetting serves its purpose in business and government to study trends. But no part of me believes that remembering the mistakes a loved one makes positively serves the relationship or family.

We are the only species on the planet that keeps punishing itself repeatedly for the same mistakes. The best gift I can give myself is to forgive and *forget* the mistakes of the past. Come to think of it, that would be one of the greatest gifts I could give anyone. It gives everyone involved the opportunities to have a fresh start each day.

I forgave by focusing on the many things that I am thankful for. I controlled my life's "cup of joy". I could not blame someone else for my unhappiness or keep looking for other people to make me happy. I had to love myself first and fill my cup with love until it overflowed. I realized my children and partner should not bear the burden of trying to fill my cup of joy. My joy is up to me and only me.

Gradually, I began to open my heart to the possibility that I could move on. I started to think about the future. But when I envisioned myself meeting someone new, I found myself wondering how I would take a new relationship to a whole new level as lots of potential pitfalls could develop early on.

I didn't pretend to know all the answers or even half of the questions, but I needed to feel that I was getting better and feeling stronger. At times I was not sure what I felt because it was all tainted with guilt, anger, hurt, and some resentment. The point was I had to feel confident that I had learned the lessons or I would risk losing more than I could ever fathom. I still reached out for Grandpa, and he continued soothing me with his reassurances that everything would be alright.

———

I was catapulted to the present by hearing a splash in the creek flowing below the bridge I was standing on. I took a deep breath. The cool fall air stung my lungs. I contemplated turning around on the trail because I knew about thirty yards down the path was a steep incline made up of over thirty steps made of railroad-ties. I decided to continue on my journey toward the stairs and slipped back into self-reflection.

EIGHT

Show and Share Your Love:
I was twenty-two years old, "in the closet", and in a two-and-a-half-year relationship with a woman. I was in sales—successful and making very good money for an early twenty-something. Through my efforts, I had earned an all-expense-paid trip to Spain of which I took full advantage...

I was surrounded by breathtaking views while I stood on the roof of a building in Spain designed by an architect named Gaudi. The world seemed to have slowed down to a snail's pace. I could hear every breath I took as the noise around me faded away. I was seeing and experiencing all these amazing things, but I was by myself. My partner could not come to Spain with me because only spouses could come and we were not open about our relationship.

At that moment, I realized I wanted more out of my life than just money, traveling, and a relationship that I could not talk to anyone about. I wanted to be in a relationship with someone who wanted to scream from the rooftops that I was hers. I didn't want to feel like she was ashamed of our relationship or that I was someone she was ashamed to be with.

Up to that moment on the rooftop, I had thought success was defined by making a lot of money, traveling, and having a nice car. I had all of these things and still felt a large void in my life. I wanted to be in a relationship I could tell the world about, but I had chosen to hide my relationship from everyone. I felt that being gay or lesbian was dangerous; that it would prevent my career from growing and cause me to lose friends and family.

That's when I heard Grandpa's voice: "Unconditional love", he said, "is the most important thing in the world—to love for love itself, with no price, no gimmick, no catch, no negotiation". It was refreshing like a cool spring rain. His words were like a comforting blanket that enveloped me in love and reassurance that wouldn't let me fall.

I knew Grandpa would be there to catch me in the same way he never let Grandma fall. Unconditional love is not about who gets more or fewer points—there is no tally at all. It's something that has no beginning or end--it's infinite. Like the horizon seen when looking across the ocean, it goes on forever—unconditional love persists no matter what.

Emotional pain comes from withholding love. It is easy to love when someone is doing what you agree with or what you want her to do. The test of unconditional love is when the person does not take the path you think she should take, but you love her even more for following her bliss.

On that rooftop in Spain, after much reflection, I made a decision that my next relationship would be with someone who was worth taking the chance of facing my fear of coming out. I wanted to walk down the street holding hands with the woman I loved. Over the next eighteen months after that day on the rooftop in Spain, a lot changed in my life. I changed careers, graduated college, ended my two-and-a-half-year in-the-closet relationship, started a new relationship with the woman who became the mother of my children, and came out to my friends and family.

This was the time when I unknowingly started doing the research that would form the foundation for this book. I started to ask Grandpa about love and relationships. I wanted to experience the kind of connection and love that my grandparents had through their marriage. Grandpa and Grandma had been married for over 58 years at the time of writing this sentence. The love they expressed toward each other throughout their lives has been a shining example for everyone who has had the fortune of meeting them.

———

About two years after Shay and I separated, during one of my visits to their house, Grandpa showed me Grandma's wedding ring. At this time Grandma was in the final stage of Alzheimer's. I had not seen the ring in many years. When Grandma started to get sick around seven years earlier, Grandpa had taken her wedding ring off for fear that it might be misplaced or lost.

As I looked at the ring, I recalled a conversation Grandma and I had had when I was a teenager. We were both sitting at the dining table and I was admiring her ring. I thought it was beautiful. I had always been a tomboy growing up, so I was never really into jewelry, but for some reason I was drawn to her wedding ring. I loved how simple yet elegant it was.

"Grandma, I think your ring is beautiful," I told her out of the blue, in between bites of my lunch. Grandma looked at me with her warm blue eyes and thanked me for the compliment. She went on to share with me how the ring came to look the way it did at that moment.

She'd originally had two rings--the wedding band and the engagement ring--but the diamond protruded in the original engagement ring. She explained how it would get caught when she put her hand in her pockets and she was afraid it would end up causing the diamond to fall out.

She and Grandpa decided to take the ring back to the jeweler they had bought the rings from in 1952. The jeweler and Grandma worked together to create a newly designed ring that combined the wedding band and engagement ring into one. That is how the ring stands right now.

As I told this story to Grandpa, his eyes began to fill with happy tears. Although, it took a lot of courage, I asked Grandpa if I could have Grandma's wedding ring. He said that he wanted to sleep on it. Months after that conversation, Grandpa called to tell me he was going to give me Grandma's wedding ring. I started to cry on the phone and told him how much it meant to me and he started to cry with me.

That ring symbolizes everything good and pure in their relationship. I felt honored that Grandpa wanted to give me Grandma's wedding ring. I could not help but think about how Grandpa has defied yet another of society's limitations. A ring often symbolized as a union between a man and a woman. "With this ring I thy wed." But yet he wanted to give her ring to me--his gay grand-daughter. This ring carries its true meaning to another generation, the true meaning of unconditional love and the commitment to love without boundaries.

———

One of many events sticks out in my mind that exemplifies how pure and honest my grandparents' love was:

About three years into our relationship, Shay and I were visiting with them. Grandma had been diagnosed with Alzheimer's four to five years earlier. She could not walk at this time and for the most part could not talk. She did not know who I was. Grandpa and my uncle were her primary caregivers.

That afternoon something moved Shay deeply about the love Grandpa showed Grandma. We were sitting with Grandma in their living room and Grandma appeared to be sleeping. For some reason I cannot recall, I got up and left the room. Grandpa walked into the room as I was walking out and he immediately walked over to Grandma and started talking to her. Shay observed the interaction between Grandpa and Grandma.

From what Shay described, Grandpa leaned over toward Grandma and said, "Donna, you are the prettiest girl I have ever seen. Do you know how much we love you?" Grandpa knelt down next to Grandma, patted her leg, held her hand, and told her, "I am so happy you are here to keep me out of trouble." With her hand in his, he stood up and gave Grandma a kiss on the cheek and then left the room.

As Grandpa was walking out I was walking back in. I looked up at Shay and noticed a tear running down her cheek. I was floored and concerned. I quickly went over to her to ask what was wrong and why she was crying. Shay said she had never seen a love like Grandpa shows Grandma. I asked her what he did or said that moved her to tears and she told me the story of what had happened. Words on paper will never be able to capture the essence of their love.

Love in many ways is the ability to see the good and "taste the sweet" in your loved one, regardless of the person's age and no matter how the years have evolved. Love is continuously melding the memory, the experience, the relevancy, and the wisdom into a sweet tenderness that keeps the relationship new and alive throughout the years.

That moment when Shay was moved to tears took on yet another meaning to me. The fact that my partner and I, an interracial same-sex couple, were sitting in my grandparents' living room was moving and inspiring. It was another example of Grandpa's unconditional love and Shay was able to experience that firsthand. Shay and I were always welcomed into their house with hugs and kisses when we arrived. Grandpa was so accepting of me, our relationship, and Shay, that he not only expressed his love for Grandma in front of Shay, but also his vulnerability. Grandpa loved Grandma in sickness and in health! And he loved me for me.

NINE

I paused on the park trail and stared at all the railroad-tie steps I needed to climb. I let out a little laugh. I looked around, but there was no one with me to share this ironic moment. I was laughing at the symbolism the stairs had in my life at that moment. I knew I could not turn back. I did not want to give up.

I started with the first step and took one step at a time. When I was halfway in my climb, I paused. I looked behind me and saw all the steps I had climbed. I looked ahead of me and saw the rest of the steps I still needed to climb. I pushed myself and finally reached the top. Even though I was short of breath, I looked back again at all the steps I had just climbed and felt a sense of accomplishment.

I rested on a bench that sat at the top of the steps overlooking the drop-off where the creek ran below. As I sat there, I recalled a walk that Shay, Jadyn, and I had taken years earlier. At this very bench, we had met a special little girl and her mother. The girl was about nine years old. She was proudly wearing a medal around her neck and walked right up to us to show us her prize.

She had won it earlier that day at the Special Olympics. Some would say this little girl looked different, but was she really any different from you and me? She craves love and acceptance. She wants to feel special. How was that any different from me? Deep in thought on the bench overlooking the creek, I heard Grandpa's voice.

Speak No Evil:

Grandpa had many verbal lessons, but one of his most profound lessons consisted not of what he said, but rather what he didn't say. One lesson that has stuck with me vividly is how he spoke of my mom—or, I should say, how he did not speak of my mom—when my parents were going through their separation.

Grandpa did not say a single mean or rude thing about my mom...*ever!* Not only did he not say a single mean thing about her, but he also would not allow anyone else to say anything rude or mean about my mom. He could have easily taken the stance of defending his son. He could have taken sides, but he said he had nothing but respect for my mom. He said that without her, he would not have had my brother and me.

I recall thinking how amazing this was, even at the age of thirteen. Grandpa saw that many people he cared about were hurting, but he did not make anyone the scapegoat. So many other people would have taken sides when they listened to someone venting their hurt feelings. He never did that. Through these actions, he taught me a critical lesson: "speak no evil". Many people link the phrase "Speak no evil" to the Three Wise Monkeys--the symbols of the "see no evil, hear no evil, and speak no evil". Our culture views this message as "turning a blind eye", or ignoring, the misconduct of others rather than exposing it.

What I took from Grandpa's lesson is that it means just what it says: "see no evil". To the extent that you have control--don't look at evil, don't watch evil, don't let evil enter your body and mind. I don't drink spoiled milk or eat rotten meat, why would I allow the emotional equivalent enter my mind and heart? If I digested spoiled milk or rotten meat, my body would need to release it quickly in some way. It's the same with evil or negativity. It is critical to release evil in some way, but for some people this release may have a negative result.

We often release negativity, or "blow off that steam", by directing it towards the people closest to us. I was guilty of doing this to Grandpa during the conversation we had that summer during my parent's separation. When we see negative or evil, we internalize it. When we internalize it, it becomes part of us. If we do not release it in a positive way, it will wreak havoc on our bodies and mind. Finding positive ways to release evil or negativity such as meditation, working out, and giving back to those in need becomes empowering--darkness and negativity disappear in the presence of light, giving back, and practicing gratitude.

In my view the next phrase, "Hear no evil", carries the same principle. When we hear evil or negativity it becomes part of us. Our mind and body absorb it like a sponge and we must release it in a positive ways so it doesn't overcome us. I believe "Speak no evil" is a little different. Seeing and hearing both involve taking something into our mind and body while speaking involves pushing something out. Speak no evil can be seen as the outcome of the other two if negativity is not released.

This lesson is not about ignoring misconduct and it is not about looking at the world through "rose-colored glasses". This lesson is about a choice I had to make. When Shay and I separated it was not just the separation of the two of us, but also of friends and families. I had to evaluate who I surrounded myself with because I was emotionally raw. I had to surround myself with positive, empowering, and loving friends and family. Through their support I was able to operate from a place of love.

I want to be the person that my children want and enjoy being around. I believe that they would want to be around someone that is positive and encouraging.

Through Grandpa's actions of "speak no evil", I have come to learn that this process starts by focusing on what is happening "in me" not what is happening around me that is out of my control. The power in driving change first starts by changing me and the meaning I place on the events in my life. If I allow negativity and fear to dominate my thoughts and feelings, I will likely attract the things I fear.

TEN

Love Yourself—Be Yourself:
In the last four years of my relationship with Shay leading up to our separation, I had gradually fallen out of love with myself. I was so focused on what I didn't have and on financial stress that I had robbed myself of joy and of being present. How could I fully love my children and someone else if I did not love myself?

———

Every self-identified gay person has a coming-out story and I am no different. One of my biggest fears is people judging me and not accepting me once they know who I truly am. Another way of putting this may be feeling like I am not enough. Writing this book and sharing it with the world has been a scary experience for me as it shows a vulnerable side of me and it puts me out there for everyone to judge.

Coming out to my dad was scary because he was the first family member I told. I asked him to drive two hours down to Columbus to talk. We went to a bar with one of his friends, who happen to be gay. After a few drinks, I mustered up the courage to tell Dad. I stumbled over my words but finally put a string of words together, "I have to tell you something. Dad, I am gay and Shay and I are in a relationship."

I held my breath as I observed his reaction. He paused for a moment and then said, "That's it?" He let out a deep breath, "I thought you were going to have bad news for me." He was completely cool with it. I immediately started to laugh and cry at the same time because I felt like a huge weight had been lifted off my shoulders. I guess the apple does not fall from tree. My dad showed the same unconditional love that Grandpa does.

Of all the people I came out to, my mom struggled the most. Because of conversations in the past, I knew she did not agree with the gay lifestyle. My mom is a very direct woman. You will always know where you stand with her, and I respect that greatly about her.

I called my mom on the phone. We had a couple of minutes of small talk and then I said, "I have something to tell you and one of two things will happen. You will either accept what I am going to tell you or you will disown me and not talk to me anymore. I have prepared myself for either decision you make."

I took a deep breath, "I am gay and Shay and I are in a relationship." She was silent on the phone. It seemed like hours of silence but it was probably just a few seconds. She gathered her thoughts and asked, "Are you sure?" "Yes, I am sure", I responded. My mom went on to explain that she loved me but she did not understand "it". Our conversation was pretty short after I told her. For many years she continued to struggle with accepting the fact that her little girl was in a same-sex relationship.

An important realization I came to while I was coming to terms with who I am is that being gay is not *my* issue. It is the none-accepting person's issue. I am not saying this to be mean or brash. I am saying it because I had come to terms with the fact that I am gay. I accepted and fell in love with that part of me and I understood that God made me perfect just the way I am. I deserved to love me for me. If someone does not love something about me that is not my issue; it is their issue and that person must find their own way of placing love above judgment. That is their journey just as I am traveling my own journey.

Five years later, after Shay and I had had a child together, my mom talked to me about her struggles with the idea of me being in a same-sex relationship. When Shay had been pregnant with our first child, Jadyn, I wondered if my mom would claim our daughter as her grand-daughter. I had prepared myself for the worst—that she would not claim Jadyn and that she would be ashamed of her granddaughter because she was a biracial child who came from artificial insemination and was carried by my partner.

I remember the first time my mom held Jadyn like it was yesterday. I saw this strong, direct woman completely melt. She had recently had surgery and I know she was in pain but my mom did not care. It was clear that she was not going to miss out on the chance of holding her two-month-old granddaughter.

Now when we arrive at events or parties, my mom comes and gets the kids and parades them around to show them off as *her* "grandbabies". She is one of the proudest grandmas I have ever seen and it is one of the most moving moments for me to see. It is a testament to what unconditional love can bring into our lives.

Everyone has "things" about themselves they either hide or show to the world. When you are gay, you can either choose to hide your sexual orientation or you can let the world know who you are. I don't believe being gay defines me as a person, but many people have or will try to define me in this one-dimensional way. God does not create one-dimensional people. I feel I have taught my family what true unconditional love is by coming out. What is unconditional love? It is love without boundaries or rules. Love without conditions. The love I have been blessed to experience through my family.

———

About two years after I came out to Grandpa, I asked him if he was still learning life lessons at the age of seventy-five and he said yes. I asked him what his most recent lesson was and he replied, "Unconditional love". I asked him what triggered the lesson and he said my coming out. He said that he wants me to be happy and he believes that the number-one thing that trumps everything in God's eyes is *love*.

What a great example Grandpa has set on all levels. Why can't we all be more like him? When are we going to stop making excuses for people from older generations who do not practice love like Grandpa does? It is a choice to hate and pass judgment on people.

Choosing love over judgment has nothing to do with someone's age or where they grew up. Who are we to play God? A person's sexual orientation should never be a reason to withhold love from someone. I have heard people say that they do not understand why someone is gay or lesbian. My response is simple: Do you understand love?

ELEVEN

I returned to Blendon Woods Park on June 17, 2013, about two-and-half-years after my separation from Shay. Accompanied by Shay, Jadyn, and Jordyn, we had gone to the park on Father's Day so the kids could each release helium-filled balloons with notes attached to them to their Papa, Tim. I didn't know it then, but that Father's Day would be the last time we would visit the park together. Something was different as if it were the closing of that chapter in my life.

A Beautiful Sunset Signals the End of the Day, but It Is Always Followed by a Breathtaking Sunrise

I am a woman in process...

It has been challenging navigating through everything that comes with separating from someone that you love, but I still hope for the best for all of us. My hopes are that Shay finds her true soul mate and I dream that one day we can put all of this behind us and be friends. I dream that one day Shay and her partner and me and my wife can have joint birthday parties and holidays together with our children.

I will always love Shay. She blessed me with two amazing gifts--our daughter and son. I have learned so much from our relationship. I am now clear about what I want and don't want out of my next relationship. I have come to understand what my "non-negotiables" are and now I can better communicate those needs. Shay was my first true love. She broke my heart wide open which enabled me to experience my life at a whole new level and for that I am thankful.

The best way to describe the sensation of being broken wide open is to compare it to a muscle that has just been pushed to the test. If you have ever studied muscle development, you know that when someone works out a muscle, it actually tears, and then in forty-eight hours, the muscle becomes stronger where it was torn. I was torn wide open, and now I am stronger in the areas where I was torn. There is a parallel between this process and life. We become stronger in the areas where we have been torn...if we allow it.

I have learned so much through this experience. Looking back on my life, I cannot see how I have learned from my successes. All of my learning and growth has come from my perceived failures. Since I learned so many things from my failures, can I really call them failures? I must be proud of my battle wounds and wear them with my head held high. My battle wounds are many— a broken relationship, four unsuccessful business attempts, and a bankruptcy,—all poor attempts at finding happiness.

Happiness is overrated. I have asked many people what they want out of life and they say, "I just want to be happy". Many times I have been asked the same question and like most, I reply, "I just want to be happy". Do any of us really know what happiness is? Do I really know what happiness is? I feel as if I have been brainwashed by society into "the pursuit of happiness"…a fairy tale. Would I rather experience happiness or be joyful? Which is more real?

In my eyes, joy and happiness are different. The problem is that most people associate happiness with outcomes or material things. Joy, however, comes from within our heart and soul. I would rather be joyful than happy any day. To me, saying I want to be happy is like chasing a ghost that I can never touch, but I can hold the hand of joy.

I believe each person must find their own way to walk hand-in-hand with joy. I found my joy by letting go and letting God and the universe do its work. I focused on serving and expressing my gratitude for the people in my life and for those who have not yet come into my life. I have also picked up a daily dose of meditation and I work out regularly.

My life has unfolded in divine order. Now I view my life in two segments: pre–*the gift* and post–*the gift*. Nothing has changed my life more profoundly than the events leading up to and including my separation. It was the hardest and most painful time of my life and yet it was the most rewarding because of all the growth and all the lessons I learned. I felt like I had been to hell and back, but now I know why I had been so unhappy. I thought I was unhappy because of what I was not getting, but in reality, I was unhappy because of what I was not giving.

I was not serving and giving to the people that surrounded me. I was not pursuing my heart's desire and what I felt I was put on this earth to do. We all have a calling. My calling is giving back to people. My duty is to give back the gift of the lessons I learned through my failures and from Grandpa. The main way I intend to give back is through my business, Poised Affluence. I have completed my coaching certification with the Robbins Madanes Center and my purpose drives me.

Through my business, I am determined to help same-sex and open-minded straight couples save their relationships so that they can in turn save their families. Another way I intend on giving back is by donating 50% of the profits from this book to a fund I will set up to perform random acts of kindness. I plan on recording those acts and posting them on a YouTube channel I created called "Grandpa's Wisdom". I will also post them on www.PoisedAffluence.com for all to view. My hopes are people will be inspired to "pay it forward".

The most important things in my life are the relationships that inspire and cultivate me as a person. Think about it: When you feel emotionally connected to your spouse, don't you feel like you can move mountains? It is no accident that when you and your spouse are in harmony and the other relationships in your life are strong, great things come into your life and are naturally attracted to you.

There were times that I felt frustrated. There was one specific conversation I had with God that sticks out in my mind. I was driving myself home from my cousin's wedding that was three-and-half hours away in Northwest Ohio. I asked God why Shay had someone in her life but I was alone.

I pleaded with God saying, "I have done the work and followed your path." I continued talking out loud almost yelling as if God were sitting in the passenger seat next to me listening--"I am ready for someone special to come into my life. I want to share my life, love, and experiences with my soul mate." I guess you could say that I was praying *boldly*.

I had that conversation with God on a Sunday and three days later I met my soul mate, Monica--the woman that I am now in a relationship with. In a conversation that Monica and I had a few weeks after we started dating, we discovered that we were both praying boldly on the same day, that exact weekend. She had asked God to bring someone special into her life and for her long-awaited family to come into her life.

My mom really likes Monica, yet in true mother fashion she advised me to take my time in this relationship. She did not want to see me get hurt again just like any mother protecting her young. My response was, "It has been about three-and-half years since I dated someone seriously. How much more time do I need to take?"

Shortly after Monica and started dating a major challenge came knocking on my door that brought me to my knees. In that moment Monica was my rock and supported me in every way. I called Grandpa to talk. In the midst of the conversation I shared the injustice I had faced with him and this is what he had to say, "I don't know how it happens but God puts the exact right people into your life at the right time." He went on to say how thankful he was that God had put Monica in my life.

TWELVE

Love Liberates:
The act of letting go is actually an act of love. Letting go is giving love the wings to be free instead of weighing it down with chains of fear. Just like a dove being released from a cage, I have spread my wings and was free. My freedom came when I stopped believing the past could have been any different.

We all have demons and things we have to face. Shay and I realized that we could not give each other what we needed and deserved. There was no fault. There was no blame. It just was. Sure, we both said and did things that were mean and hurtful during the separation process, but just as Anne Frank said, "Despite everything, I believe that people are really good at heart." Everything happened the way it was intended to happen. I would not be where I am right now, nor would I be the person and parent I have become without everything happening exactly the way it happened.

Given what I have gone through in the past few years, why I am not cynical? Why have I not given up on love and on finding my soul mate? Well, I recall hearing an interesting take on cynicism that put it in perspective for me:

Cynicism is not wisdom.
Cynicism masquerades as wisdom.
Cynicism is a self-imposed blindness.

We put blinders on ourselves to protect us from a world that we think may hurt us or disappoint us. We live blinded in fear. I dare you to be brave! Believe things will be good. I dare you to open your heart to love again! The greatest gift we have been given is to love. We feel our deepest pain when we withhold love.

I cannot think of a better example of this than my mom coming to terms with the fact that I will never marry a man and that her two grandchildren came from a same-sex relationship. If she would have withheld love because of an old, ignorant, worn-out belief system, she would have missed out on all the memories and experiences with me and her two grandchildren that adore her. I see my mom light up when Jadyn and Jordyn run up to her and give her hugs--a shining example of the purest form of love.

After only a few months of meeting Monica, mom invited her to a family function and for the first time ever referred to my significant other as "my girlfriend" She asked me over the phone so she could not see the look on my face but I lit up.

It was the first time that I felt like my mom was not ashamed of whom I was or who I was with. She was placing love above judgment and no longer cared what others thought or felt about her daughter being in a same-sex relationship. For the first time in years, I felt like my mom loved me unconditionally. It felt like a weight was lifted from our shoulders and a sense of freedom washed over both of us. The cage of fear and cynicism had been removed from our relationship.

It is better to be hurt than to not believe in love. I will never give up on love because love is what I am. I will be open to whatever God's plan is for me. My life is in God's hands. I am just going to enjoy the ride. The quality of my life is in direct relation to the level of uncertainty I can comfortably live with.

It is amazing looking back on my life events. There was a time after my separation that I questioned and could not imagine ever being in another relationship. Shay and I never had a ceremony I have always wanted to experience my wedding ceremony with a woman I am completely in love with.

I recall a specific conversation with my best friend, Hilary, about a year-and-half ago. During lunch with Hilary, I told her how I didn't think I could ever see myself getting married or having a wedding. Her advice to me was simple--stay open to all possibilities. Who knows? Maybe someday my childhood dream will be coming true as I watch Monica walk down the aisle toward me in her wedding gown. Just maybe my mom will be sitting in the front row crying tears of joy because she is so happy for her daughter and her daughter's dreams coming true. Maybe Grandpa would be sitting next to her with a smile on his face and joy in his heart.

Wouldn't that be a magic moment? Mom--a country girl from a small, rural town raised in the 60's and Grandpa--a man in his 80's born during the depression, both sitting in the front row of a same-sex wedding supporting from a place of pure unconditional love. This is true freedom!

One day during one of our many long conversations, Monica said something very beautiful to me. It was so profound, yet so simple. She said, "Am I going to choose to walk in fear or am I going to choose to walk in faith and love?" This is a question we all need to ask ourselves. What path are you going to choose?

THIRTEEN

One of the greatest enigmas puzzling the human race is what the secret of a good life is. That rhetorical question, posed by countless people over countless years, will seemingly keep people looking for answers. Grandpa says the path to happiness and joy is counting your blessings, showing gratitude, and thanking God for the many gifts you have been given—and doing these things every day, not just when things are challenging. I would like to add another element: letting go, not trying to control everything, and allowing God to show you the path instead of forcing yourself down a path.

The Secret to the Good Life:

Grandpa's wisdom is much like God's love. It is in everyone and around everyone, if we choose to surrender to lessons and love.

I think I have figured out the secret to the good life. Grandpa certainly has figured it out. He has taught me many lessons that I have described in this book. But there is one additional lesson that is the catalyst to make all the other lessons a part of who you are and what you will be remembered for. That lesson is that you should take the initiative to express your love and gratitude to all people who you have in your life. Pay it forward.

The day I figured out the secret to the good life, I deliberately chose to practice Grandpa's lesson about love and gratitude. I called my dad and thanked him for being an amazing dad. My dad told me that it made his day; I told him that it was only 9:14 a.m., and the sky was the limit for the day. I called my mom and thanked her for being an amazing mother. Then I called Grandpa and thanked him for being a wonderful grandpa.

The next short conversation I had with Grandpa made the light bulb go off for me. After I told him thank you, he said, "You are welcome." I could hear how proud he was of me through the phone. He went on to say, "This is what I have always preached to you."

As I spoke to Grandpa this morning, he told me that he was sitting next to "a beautiful young lady". He told her how excited he was to spend the day with her, and that he is so thankful she is here so he can pester her. Grandpa said Grandma gave him a million-dollar smile.

Grandma had been bedridden for thirty-two months because of Alzheimer's. She cannot talk and cannot feed herself. She sometimes has a hard time eating. Grandpa's true love, his wife, his best friend, his lover, the person he has grown old with, has been slowly taken from him by this awful disease. Through the phone I could feel Grandpa's happiness and gratitude that he could spend another day with Grandma.

You see, Grandpa makes a choice every day. He could choose to be mad at God for allowing this to happen to the woman he loves so deeply, or he could live his life with gratitude and drink up every last moment he has with the people around him. Grandma has had Alzheimer's for over ten years. If he had lived his life in bitterness, frustration, or sadness, those emotions would have muted his enjoyment of so many things, including ten years' worth of exciting moments and experiences, like the birth of four great-grandchildren.

What Grandpa was talking about is paying it forward, passing it along. What is *it*? Love, appreciation, a helping hand, a patient ear, a shoulder to cry on, unconditional love, gratitude, lessons learned...telling people that you love them and care about them, and being there to support them while you are here, instead of when it is too late. I cannot give those things when I am gone, and neither can you. Shay's mom taught me a saying that expresses this sentiment well: "Give people their flowers when they are here."

On December 12, 2013 Donna "Grandma" Jean Blasiman passed away. I interviewed Grandpa for this book about three months after she passed. The inspiring interview can be viewed at www.poisedaffluence.com/books. In the video he shares the lessons on how important it is to tell everyone you love that you love them. Don't wait until it is too late and they are gone. Grandpa talks about how hard it was watching the undertakers carry Grandma out of the house. The house they had spent the better part of a sixty year marriage together. That would be the last time Grandpa and Grandma would be in the house together. Give your love openly and freely. The greatest pain is not from being hurt, but from withholding love.

What is the secret to the good life?

Giving and receiving love and gratitude openly and freely.

This is something I have been practicing. No one snaps his or her fingers and lives in gratitude. It takes discipline and practice to live in a continual state of gratitude. But that is the state that Grandpa operates in 24/7.

We choose what to focus on. We choose how to interpret the meaning of life events. We have a choice as to whether the world happens to us or whether we happen to the world. What will be your choice? I have made mine! And I will continue to practice that decision and pay my gift forward until the day I die.

Appreciation of what you have brings what you want!

—

I just walked out of Jadyn and Jordyn's room. They move me to tears of joy. There is so much I don't understand with my head but feel perfectly with my heart. Only the logic of the heart can put it all together. I am not sure what tomorrow will bring or how long God plans on me being on this earth. My gratitude for life—my life—is present now. I have asked myself what I want to be remembered for when my time here on this earth is done.

I want to be remembered as an advocate for same-sex couples, singles, and families. I want to be remembered for being an amazing wife, a daughter my parents are proud of, and a sister who can always be counted on. I want to be remembered as an amazing parent to my two children. I want to be their hero, their "Grandpa." I want to lead the life my children aspire to have and be the person my children aspire to become. I want to make a difference in people's lives. I want to matter. I want to be loved, not just recalled.

My attitude reflects my presence and my commitment to living in gratitude and love. Ralph Waldo Emerson may have said it best, "Success: To laugh often and much, to win the respect of intelligent people and the affection of children, to appreciate beauty, to find the best in others, to leave the world a bit better, whether by a healthy child, garden patch, or a redeemed social condition, to know even one life has breathed easier because you have lived. This is to have succeeded."

I wish you all peace, harmony, laughter, and love.

Dare to love again.

CPSIA information can be obtained at www.ICGtesting.com
Printed in the USA
LVOW04s1439180615

442982LV00018B/624/P